Passive Income Techniques

Proven Strategies to Generate Passive Income and Gain Financial Freedom

Sarah Carter

All Rights Reserved worldwide. No part of this publication may be reproduced in any form or by any means, including scanning, photocopying, or otherwise without prior written permission of the copyright holder.

Copyright © 2020 Hook Heath Publishing

www.hookheathpublishing.com

About the Author – Sarah Carter

An ex-model that went on to become a successful freelance consultant in the financial services industry.

The books are based on the techniques used over the years in business working as a consultant.

It is deliberate the books are not too long, but sufficient to give you a background into the subject. After all, 'Brevity is the soul of wit', William Shakespeare.

I'd love to your story. My email is
Sarah@hookheathpublishing.com

Table of Contents

About the Author – Sarah Carter 3

Introduction 5

Selling Your Knowledge 7

Renting your Property 11

Online Paid Advertising 13

Affiliate Marketing 14

Investing in Stocks and Shares that Pay Dividends 16

Using High Interest Savings Accounts 19

Investing in Real Estate Investment Trusts .. 23

Making Use of Your Free Space 25

Selling Stock Photos 27

Creating a Blog 29

Conclusion 33

Introduction

A passive income strategy is where you continue to receive returns on your work or investment with minimal or no ongoing effort. There may be scope to increase your passive income from a particular source by repeating the process with additional effort or investment.

You can also increase your returns by adopting multiple passive income strategies. This has the additional benefit of reducing your risk by not being dependent on one strategy for all your passive income.

There are many different sources of passive income to consider. Some strategies will require start-up cash whereas others just require your time and effort. If you do not have the time to adopt a passive income strategy, you can consider outsourcing the work. It may well be outsourcing leads to a better end result and may also enable you to take on tasks that you are not comfortable doing yourself.

A passive income strategy may start as a way to supplement your income, but can grow to replace your existing income or job. There are many different reasons a passive income strategy is attractive. Some people are bored with their existing job, some people want to spend more time with friends and family and others may want to spend more time travelling to new destinations. Whatever your reason, there will be a passive

This book is intended to inspire you to consider a passive income strategy. This will be done by providing examples of proven strategies and useful advice for implementing the strategies.

Selling Your Knowledge

If you think hard enough, everyone has a passion, experience or understanding of a subject that would be of interest to other people. Such knowledge of facts, skills or subject matter is a valuable resource that can be converted into passive income.

Furthermore, such knowledge can be gained or expanded upon using many different methods. These methods could include reading books, searching the internet for articles or videos, watching television documentaries, attending lectures, visiting museums, talking to subject matter experts or education.

Whichever approach you take (and there could be several), remember to make extensive notes in a notebook or computer.

You are unlikely to use all the information you gather, but if unsure, write it down anyway.

The next step is to organise your notes into different categories and remove any duplicates. Remember to capture any examples that validate the facts in your notes.

Once you have the knowledge you can set about converting it into passive income. A common place to start is to convert the knowledge into a book.

The reason why we split the research into categories is because these will become chapters in your book. If you decide the knowledge in the book logically falls into separate groups of categories, you may consider splitting the research into two or more books.

The book could either be a in a digital format (e.g. an eBook), a physical format (e.g. a paperback or hardback). Start with an eBook and then it is quite a quick task to convert it into a paperback as well.

Remember the books can be sold into multiple countries and/or translated into multiple languages.

Audiobooks are becoming more popular but require more financial investment as you need to use a professional narrator.

Another passive income stream to consider for your knowledge is an online training course.

Also consider outsourcing some of the work to third parties, which will increase the costs but may prove cost effective.

When considering outsourcing, you need to consider if you have the skills to do the task yourself to the same standard. However, another technique is to put a value on your own time. If the cost of outsourcing the work is less than the value you put on your own time, this is another indication that outsourcing is a sensible option.

Once the book is written and published, you will have a passive income stream with a minimal financial outlay. However, you will find the time and effort required is considerable, particularly with your first few books. But when you consider you can earn as much as 70% commission on anything you sell it becomes an attractive source of passive income.

Be aware that Amazon will check to see if any content is freely available anywhere on the internet and copying other people's books is likely to have copyright implications. If Amazon believe you are breaching their rules, they are unlikely to publish your book and likely to close your account.

The best place to start is the Amazon KDP platform. This is free to join and provide lots more training, such as choose the right books to sell.

Remember the quality of your book be reflected in your sales as online reviews are so important.

Renting your Property

Another common source of passive income is rental properties. However, there are some risks to consider with this method.

- Does the rental income on your property make this an attractive proposition?
- What are the likely costs you expect to pay (both initial and ongoing) that will reduce your overall return on the rental property?
- What other risks are associated with this method, including periods when the property is vacant and not generating an income and repair/maintenance costs that were not anticipated associated with the property?

It is recommended that you are honest with yourself when estimating the returns on this strategy. Do your research and maybe come up with best-case and worst-case scenarios. Talk to rental agents and look online.

Typically, it is recommended to present the property in good condition, as this will be more appealing to potential clients and a client is more likely to look after the property better. However, do not spend too much on the property as this will affect your future returns.

Also, take into consideration that the value of the property will change over time (either as an increase or decrease in value). Furthermore, your money will be tied up in the property until it is sold and there will also be costs associated with selling the property.

For both reasons, the property should be seen as a long-term strategy.

Online Paid Advertising

Online Advertising, in this context, is where you are paid passive income to rent space on your websites or social media accounts. Therefore, people who want to advertise their product or service will pay you if someone performs a specific action (e.g. clicking on a link or banner) that redirects the visitor from your website or social media account to one owned by the person renting the space from you.

In simple terms, the advertiser is paying you to send internet traffic to their offer. This works best if your website or social media account is receiving a high volume of visitors, ranks well in the search engines and the content is relevant to the advertiser. For example, an advertiser selling wedding dresses is not going to pay to advertise on a website about dog food!

Affiliate Marketing

Affiliate marketing is similar to paid advertising and another way to generate passive income if you have a relevant website to your advertiser.

Note, social media accounts are less likely to accept direct links to an affiliate advertiser's website as they are more interested in keeping visitors on their social media website. However, you can place links on social media accounts to your own website and include affiliate marketing links or banners on your website.

Affiliate marketing works by a person visiting your website clicks on an affiliate's link or banner and goes on to make a purchase. This could either be a 'one off' payment or a regular payment if the customer purchases a product that requires a monthly payment.

Again, you need your website to be relevant to the affiliate and have a high volume of visitors to make this a viable passive income strategy.

There will be some ongoing effort required with this method to update the content of the website on a regular basis to keep customer coming back to your website and attract new ones. Remember to post links on your social media accounts to increase awareness of the new article and encourage people to like and share the post to generate more traffic to your website.

Your website is not directly about selling anything, just keeping your visitors interested so they visit again. Choose a subject you are passionate about and write high quality original content.

This is a low risk, low cost strategy but it does require some ongoing effort.

Investing in Stocks and Shares that Pay Dividends

A dividend is a passive income payment made pro-rata by a company to its shareholders as a share of the profits earned in over a set period of time. A company will typically pay a dividend twice a year, but they may choose to pay more or less dividends in a year, including none at all.

If a company does not pay of its profits in dividends in a year, the surplus is retained in the company and can be included in dividend payments in future years. If a company has made a loss in the year and has no retained earnings it cannot pay a dividend until the company returns to profitability. Once you have purchased your shares, you will receive any dividends with no additional effort for as long as you own the shares. However, there is a cut off date for each dividend and you must own the shares on that date to be entitled to that dividend.

You will need to do some research before you buy shares in a company. This will include looking at historical dividend payments and share prices and any press articles to check the company is in good health and its future prospects.

Consider buying your stocks or shares through an Investment fund. In this way your investment will be pooled with lots of other investors and invested in a wide range of suitable stocks or shares. The fund will be managed by a professional fund manager who will be supported by a large number of additional staff to perform such activities as research and preparing accounts. The fund manager will also meet with the directors of the company on a regular basis, so will have a good insight into the health of the company and their future plans.

There are different types of funds with different investment objectives. Furthermore, there are different ways to invest in the fund that will have different tax advantages. These will vary by country, so again you will need to do your research. Also look at the charges payable on these investments. For example, Exchange Traded Funds (known as ETFs) if available tend to have lower charges than some other types of fund.

Although the risk of the funds is reduced by spreading the investment across multiple stocks and shares, there is still a risk the value of the fund will decrease.

The best way to mitigate against a fall in the value of stocks or shares or investment funds is to trat these as long-term investments. Also, it is wise to keep some cash in reserve, so you are not forced to sell these investments at short notice as this is where you are more likely to make a loss on your investment.

Using High Interest Savings Accounts

Possibly the most passive income strategy! This could either be a single lump sum transfer of cash or a regular transfer of cash, say monthly. Even the latter can be automated so there is no additional effort and you are more likely to forget or be tempted to avoid making the transfer in a particular month.

As ever, you need to do your research to select the savings account paying the best interest rates. For example, an online savings account may pay better returns and look at the frequency of when the interest is paid i.e. the sooner the interest is in your account, the sooner you start earning interest on a larger amount. Also look at the terms of the savings account. For example, some savings accounts may pay higher interest rates but not allow you access to the cash for a fixed period of time or only permit a limited number of withdrawals, say per year.

Like with other strategies in this book, the more cash you put in, the greater the returns. Also, the longer the cash is in the savings account, the greater the overall returns. Therefore, the sooner you start the better, even a child could do it and it is good practice to start generating passive income as early as possible.

It is important to confirm the savings account is approved by the local regulator in your country. This mean there will be a maximum limit for the savings account and providing the total saving remain below that limit, your savings are protected. Therefore, this is one of the lowest risk strategies but the returns are likely to be lower that some of the other strategies.

The only problem that might arise if the economy weakens. In that case, the interest rates will tend to drop and you won't get as much of a pay-out as you would otherwise.

Check the terms of the account as to whether the interest rate is fixed for a period or varies depending on the overall interest rate in your country. A fixed rate interest savings account provides certainty for a period of time as the interest rate will not fall. However, conversely if the overall country interest rate rises, you will not receive a higher interest rate for the for the term of the Fixed rate account.

Not directly related to passive income strategies, but if you have outstanding debts, you may wish to consider paying these off more quickly, providing there is no penalty for taking this approach.

In addition, you may wish to consider reviewing how you spend your money each month. This is best done by looking at your bank statements and credit card statements.

Make a list of the types of payment and the amount spent and ask yourself 'did I really need to spend that money?' and 'Are there cheaper options?'. If you spend less, you can put more money into your high interest savings account.

By spending money on cards, even small amounts, rather than cash you will have a better understanding of how you spend your money each month.

You can also dig deeper and look at itemised bills, like you weekly food shop to see if it can be reduced. Maybe look at alternative supermarkets to compare prices and consider splitting your food shopping between multiple supermarkets.

Consider online shopping and having your food delivered. Not only will this save you time and travel costs, it will also reduce the risk of impulse purchases.

Investing in Real Estate Investment Trusts

Real Estate Investment Trust (REITs) are like a fund as discussed earlier in this book where the investment strategy is usually to purchase a share of multiple commercial properties. The investment strategy of a particular REIT will normally focus on a particular type of commercial property. For example, care homes, shopping centres or hotels.

Like with Income funds, you will receive dividends if the REIT generates a profit.

In terms of value, this type of investment is probably the largest by value. However, the value of commercial property in many sectors is in decline due to the state of the world economy and the move towards online shopping.

However, sectors such as hospitals or care homes are one of the few exceptions due to the ageing population and the current threat from the COVID 19 virus.

Because of the nature of the investments, sometimes a REIT or an Exchange Traded Fund invested in REITs may suspend withdrawals for a period of time.

AT this point in time in 2020, this is probably one of the highest risk strategies discussed in this book. I have left it in this book as it has been such a large source passive income and rising values in the past. Furthermore, everything has a price so there will still be opportunities in this strategy. For example, in some cases the land might be worth more than the commercial properties, so there may be scope to develop the land or change the use of commercial properties, say to residential properties.

Certainly not to consider unless you really know this sector well and not for the inexperienced investor.

Making Use of Your Free Space

Many people have a spare bedroom in their house where mostly it is just used to store items that you probably do not use or need anymore.

With a bit of effort, this room could be cleared and a lot of the items either thrown away, moved somewhere else or even sold.

Then freshen up the room with a coat of paint, maybe a new carpet and curtains and some basic bedroom furniture. Then you have a room you can rent out on websites like Airbnb. Alternatively, you could rent the room out on a monthly basis which might be less ongoing effort to generate passive income.

Taking this idea further, the space does not need to be a room. It could be a driveway, a garage or even space in shed. A friend of mine has a large field behind her house that she rents out to campers and another allows a field to be used to exercise horses. I also know a farmer who allows a mobile phone mast to be located on his land.

When you have a few ideas, as with renting a property, you need to do your research.

- How much Income could I generate?
- What would be the ongoing costs and effort?
- What other risks are involved?

In addition, you also need to check if you are legally allowed to do and whether you need planning permission.

Insurance will be another factor to make sure you are still covered.

Selling Stock Photos

Stock photographs is where high quality photographs you have taken and placed under copyright are made available for use by customers in return for the payment of a licence fee. The licence will detail the usage rights of how the photograph can and cannot be used.

Example of usage rights may include –

- Commercial and non-commercial use.
- Usage may include websites, newspapers, book covers or content, Clothing etc.
- The right to edit the photograph
- The right to share or sell the photograph to a third party.

Typically, the photographs are displayed for sale including a watermark of the seller or agency which is only removed on purchase.

So, if you are a keen photographer, this might be an option for you to generate a passive income.

I live a few minutes' walk from a nice beach, which often generates opportunities for great photographs.

Take a look at some of the stock photo websites for inspiration.

The photographs can be sold in many different ways. A popular approach is to register the photographs with some of the largest stock photo agencies who will pay you a commission each time your photograph is purchased.

Similar opportunities exist for video footage, original music, graphic design images etc.

Creating a Blog

The term blog comes from an abbreviation of the term weblog. It is a type of website that provides information and encourages discussion usually on a particular subject.

The blog is updated on a regular basis with text-based articles (known as posts) where the latest article appears at the top of the web page.

More recently a video post-based version of blogs has emerged known as vlogs and sometimes the two types of post are combined.

The process of updating a blog is known as blogging. The process is often combined with social media accounts or even performed exclusively on social media accounts.

The concept is not to sell anything on the Blog but to provide useful, interesting information so that the blog generates a following of people that have a common interest in the content of the blog. If they like what they read they will check back to the blog on a regular basis. They are also likely to like and share the posts on their own social media accounts. This also leads to more readers and followers.

Once the readers start to 'know like and trust' you it is possible to find ways to redirect your readers to affiliate offers. However, this is best done in subtle ways so the primary focus of the blog remains as providing information, not just going straight for the hard sell.

Once you have a large following you can partner with other companies to provide content to your followers in return for a fee or revenue share. i.e. you are driving website traffic to a partner's website in return for a fee.

Sometimes blogs are used to review products that may be of interest to your readers. The review then redirects them to where they can buy the product. A similar process can be used to direct customers to buy your own products.

You may wish to add adverts onto your blog such that you receive a commission when the ad is seen or clicked on.

It maybe you offer premium content to subscribers who have joined your mailing list or paid a VIP membership fee.

Blogs are also incredibly popular with website search engines, as these websites generate a lot of visitors, provide relevant and regularly updated content. That ticks a lot of boxes with the likes of Google.

The opportunities are endless. Building up a following on your blog can take time and a lot of effort. Like with book writing, the blog will only be as successful as the quality of the content. Set yourself a goal to update your blog with a new post, ideally once a day. You can always write multiple posts and then release them on future dates.

Consider where in the world your audience resides and try sending the posts at different times of the day to establish which posts get the most readers.

Conclusion

The idea of this book was to introduce you to the concept of passive income. The concept is to break away from being entirely dependent on an hourly wage and start generating an income that will support you for years to come.

There is no reason why you cannot start some of these strategies alongside your day job.

Everyone's circumstances and priorities are different. Everyone's attitude to risk is different. Some people have cash to invest whereas others have spare time on their hands (or a combination of the two).

Don't be afraid to start small. It could be as simple as starting a regular savings account for one of your children (or grandchildren).

At the time of writing in 2020, a child's regular savings account can be opened with just £10 a month and receive an annual return of 4%. This can be topped up at any time up to £100 a month. Therefore, if started from birth a 15 year old child could have £6000 cash and receive a passive income on their birthday every year which at current rates would be £240.

Don't be afraid to try different strategies or even multiple strategies. For example, you could use the income from your saving account to buy more shares.

I wish you every Success!
Sarah

www.ingramcontent.com/pod-product-compliance
Lightning Source LLC
Chambersburg PA
CBHW031515210526
45464CB00007B/2928